GW00382867

contemporary haibun

Volume 4

Edited by

Jim Kacian
Bruce Ross
Ken Jones

Red Moon Press

contemporary haibun
Volume 4

Published by
Red Moon Press
PO Box 2461
Winchester VA
22604-1661 USA
redmoon shentel.net

ISBN 1-893959-34-1

Cover painting:
Mark Rothko, *Untitled*, 1950, oil on canvas.
Used by permission.

RED
MOON
PRESS

Why *Contemporary Haibun?*

In our first year or two, our serial name *American Haibun &
Haiga* (AHH) did more than yield a pleasing acronym—it also
represented well the range of our contributors and the models
used in both our featured artforms. But as the series has grown,
this has changed. A quick look through the indices of our two most
recent volumes suggests that, while the United States still
remains home to the majority of these artists, a sizable minority
has emerged from the United Kingdom, Australia, Canada—as
well as India, Romania, Croatia, even Japan. *American* simply
doesn't capture the breadth of practice which haibun and haiga
in English currently enjoy.

More difficult was dropping *haiga* from our series title. Due
to constraints of costs and technical matters, the haiga featured
in these volumes have had significant limitations, the greatest of
which is that they are produced in gray scale only, not in the color
in which many originally were executed. Even though we take
pains to select only haiga that we feel reproduces to good effect
in gray scale, there is still some loss of power and impact in these
works. On the other hand, we feel that the inclusion of haiga to
these volumes makes them distinctive; indeed, there is no other
vehicle anything quite like them. So we have opted to continue to
offer haiga, but to de-emphasize its role in the serial title. We
are pleased that other venues for full-color presentation of haiga
are becoming available, especially the *Haiga Online* site edited
by an'ya (<www.haigaonline.com>) and a new annual volume
of haiga to be edited by the well-known artist Jeanne Emrich.

In this current volume, you will find an even broader range of subject matter, styles and models of both haibun and haiga. This is due in part, no doubt, to our casting a broader net, but also to the fact that more cultures are aware of, and as a result more poets are experimenting with, these arts tangential to haiku. As we share these differing models of what works well within these varied traditions, we come to discover not only what might work in our own culture, but also are called upon to expand our way of thinking to accomodate these differences. Simultaneously, we come to realize that much of the subject matter, and our responses to it, which is shared in this way is held in common. In other words, in our differences we discover our similarities, and find mutual means of sharing them. This is no mean accomplishment, if we compare it to the international strife which seems to characterize our present world situation.

There is no doubt that haibun and haiga are growing quickly. In this, our fourth year, we considered five times as many pieces as we did for our first volume. Talks and workshops on haibun and haiga are featured at virtually every haiku conference now. International haibun contests have been created, and renewed interest in the form as it appears in classical Japanese literature is evidenced by new translations and scholarly works. Volumes of haibun by individual practitioners, many of whom will be found in these pages, now appear with regularity. The internet features many sites which offers one or both of these forms. And haibun has become a staple of readings by haiku poets worldwide.

What will become of haibun and haiga? You will decide, and on the early evidence, you have decided that these special means to elucidate the intuitive, the insightful, the profound, have a viability which ensures their continued practice for a long time to come.

The Editors

contemporary haibun

::: Luis Cuauhtémoc Berriozabál

Tales of the Dark Horned Frog

MY MOTHER IS PRACTICING VOODOO on me. She might as well be dead. That black magic is against everything God teaches. She and father worship the dark horned frog. If you don't have faith in God you might as well be destroyed. They have conspired with the Los Angeles Police Department and this psychiatric institution to put me away for a very long time. They claim I am a Schizo- phrenic. They do not understand what is going on inside me. It's the voodoo working me over. But I am strong in my faith and I'll crush them with the help of The Almighty.

> The dark horned frog
> Leaps into the pond
> Horns first

I have studied law and I will be my own lawyer. I'll bring my parents, the cops, and the mental health system on their knees for doing this to me. They'll drop their silly motion and shy away from witchcraft and back into the light. I hear God all the time. I talk to Him. He is in my corner. Psychiatric medication is the devil's chemistry. I will not take one drop, one tablet, or one shot. If they want a fight, I will give it to them.

> In the pond
> One horn out of water
> One horn submerged . . .

Luis Cuauhtémoc Berriozábal :::

Tiny Robot

THERE SEEMS TO BE SOMETHING growing in my belly. The doctor claims that I am pregnant. But I know better. This is not a child and it is not even human. I suspect it is not even of this earth. I am not speaking about aliens and I'm not sure if it comes from underground, where the dark one counts his riches in souls. I feel it is a tiny robot: something computerized, a different, smarter component that does not have a father.

I believe a virus has impregnated me. I was on-line in the "alone at home" chat room. There was another person on-line, Virusian. It asked all sorts of questions. Virusian wanted to know about my love life, if I was active in the social realm, if I was hard up. I told Virusian it was none of his or hers or its business. The questions kept coming, intrusive, demanding, and with specific commands.

I tried getting off-line. I tried turning off the computer. I pressed every button and nothing happened. I couldn't even get off the chair or look away from the screen. I was transfixed, hypnotized, glued to the screen by a force much stronger than myself. I never felt anything so powerful. It was at this point that Virusian said something would grow inside of me that would revolutionize the way children are born. Only this is not a child growing inside me, but a virus, a tiny robot.

It may look a lot like a baby to the doctor on the ultrasound. But I know better. I've had nightmares of a tiny baby robot growing inside of me for the past two weeks. This is some kind of sign. I don't understand why I'm being questioned and looked at as if I've lost my sanity. I feel perfectly fine. The only problem is this tiny robot growing inside my belly. I know the story sounds farfetched. But when it is born, I will be redeemed.

A newborn child screams
The doctor cuts
The electrical chord

Janice Bostok :::

Pre-Dawn in Tecuci

1 lying awake in pre- dawn grey we listen to the staccato voices of farm workers leaving the city to work the communal farms a clip clop of horses' hooves penetrates thin morning air and coughing tractors pulling trailer- loads of men sitting in rows on long wooden benches move farther away as i curve into your back thankful that you will not leave me alone in this foreign city a nightmare which for ever plagues me when we travel

2 in my dream you turn calling to me just as the labourer who leaves home in all seasons calls as he retreats beyond the yard beyond the gate beyond the far bend in the long long road i hear my voice echo unable to respond to the rising sun a warmth not found in the empty house now that you have gone

3. a crow slips into
the distant pine tree through
a broken branch
so easily calling
to its mate as it arrives

The Homecoming

when ready each traveller turns back as a cow does from distant pastures at milking time instinctively with a bovine devotion once the decision has been made

on any one day a forward thrust is seduced by adventures which may possibly be found around the corner of each new day

overnight the facing home looms large and necessary a plodding which quickens towards the ending of the trip

it takes time to return home from a journey for days afterwards my mind still weaves along country roads which join the state highways which then become motorways which quickly lead into the city to end in front of the airport joining the tracks of humanity slowly moving towards the check- in counters waiting at customs then being abruptly herded onto the plane

while my body sits in limbo in economy class my memory is laidback in a friend's car being driven carefully through the streets of a seaside town or smoothly on sealed roads past vineyards towards lunch at the winery or perhaps on excursion into the mountains or along the coast road towards another town

the excitement of unfamiliar scenes runs high

it takes time for me to reclaim that unfamiliar territory which i must once again call my home

returning home —
plump jacaranda blossoms
hold firm before
the rainy season weakens
their faded purple hold

::: Yvonne Cabalona

Deep Winter

In the late 80s, toward the end of a course on human sexuality I was taking, our instructor told us she was inviting a young man afflicted with AIDS to address the next session. Several class-mates chose not to attend, including a young pregnant woman who felt that breathing the same air as the AIDS victim was dangerous and could cause her to lose her baby.

I don't remember his name or where he said he was from. It was evident he had once been a very handsome young man. He never took off his coat, despite the room's warmth. He told us he would answer any questions we had except those regarding his family—he had been disowned. His eyes stared a bit blankly. His dark hair was dishevelled and graying. His vulnerability was palpable.

We knew AIDS was fatal; our curiosity was in homosexuality. We asked about that. When he spoke of San Francisco, a smile lit his thin face, the only one he showed.

Listening to his tale, a fear suddenly came over me—I had a cold. I realized he was more in danger of catching my virus than I was of catching his.

> deep winter
> I time my breathing
> with his

Yvonne Cabalona :::

Her Jeans

It was in the dim street light that I saw her. The day's warmth belied the coming cold of night, and there she was, dressed in those low- rise jeans with the built- in worn look that's so trendy right now. Because of the lighting, all of her seemed to be in shadow except her pants. I watched as she strolled further up the street, her denims moving in and out of darkness.

> early nightfall
> the tightness
> of the hooker's jeans

Peppered Mackerel

This morning I take the rest of the peppered mackerel from the fridge and place it between thick buttered slices of the bread I mixed last night. I could smell the bread when I woke and decided on the mackerel in the shower. Two sandwiches, each cut into two slabs, wrapped in clingfilm, and placed crosswise in the Tupperware box. I wipe the mackerel grease from my fingers and add an apple, a pear and the folding picnic knife, two small pieces of June's Florentine cake, wrapped in clingfilm, two paper towels folded, and the box is full. I place it in the red bag beside the old blue vacuum flask filled with instant coffee and milk and our lunch is complete.

In half-an-hour we'll meet by your office in the university and drive up through the trees, past the cemetery, to the car park above the city, the harbour and the ocean. We will talk a little about the weather, the ships in port, and how each of our days is going. When that is done, I will open the red bag and take the blue flask because that's a 'boy job'. With a laugh you will take the Tupperware box and quietly say "What have we got today?" In a few moments you will tell me how much you like the sandwiches, you will drink the coffee I've poured for you, and we will talk of things yet to come.

> late autumn light—
> a small blue sailboat passes
> from warehouse to warehouse

Tom Clausen :::

Middle Way

At times it's hard to know whether to laugh or cry. The struggle to be, just to exist requires each of us to be true to too many things to make sense of which one is right.

> a few graves apart:
> neighbors who had nothing to say
> to each other

Pencils

To this day I keep many more pencils than I need or use. Beside the computer at home and at work, beside the bed I keep them as practical artifacts of a former self and simpler time. In elementary school I began a pencil collection and by middle school I had become known as the pencil kid. I studied the various brands enough to recognize the unique patterns in the little metal tops that hold the eraser. Friends would approach me and hold out a pencil with just the head visible for me to guess the brand name. Some of my favorites were Venus Medalists, Ticonderogas, Eberhard Faber Mongols, Herald Square Mallards and Mohicans by Empire. My collection grew with a certain idiosyncratic reputation. The days of Bic pens, fountain pens and then keyboards came yet I've never been able to view any pencil as anything but a link to those days then and that special meaning in my heart.

> high school bully—
> holding the pencil out at arms length
> before snapping it

David Cobb :::

A Hole with a View

> with a ball of string
> the sexton measures sunlight
> into portions

I CAN WORK OUT MORE OR LESS where it will be. The 'old half' of the village churchyard, downside of the bank which in gently undulating Essex is styled a 'cliff', on the church side of the brook, admits no new corpses. Nowadays we villagers, when we are 'spent', recongregate on the top shelf in strict rotation. Guess how many years you may have left to live, multiply this by the average number of burials a year (five or six), and this again by six for the allowance of feet. Then, using eye or foot, you can roughly pace out the distance to your final resting place.

Mine won't be right up teetering on the cliff edge, for this position is kept for leftovers of cremations. A choice predicament. Not because the cliff has a better share of sunshine, or is nearer the sturdy support of oaks and chestnuts, or closer to birdsong in the branches or to the bells that ring for weddings, or because the moles do not riddle there. Simply, the cliff is the dress circle for viewing the gathering of the whole village on Christmas Eve for carols by candlelight. Looking over the headstones of the ancient squirearchy, one might see the silhouettes of those who will one day join one in the Land of Moles. Or at least feel the tremor of their pattering feet. A vague comfort.

> how urgently
> the gardener fills the can
> with his own water

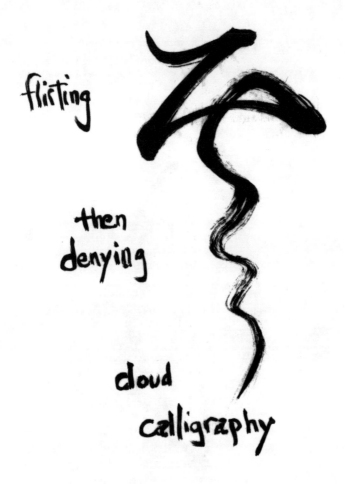

flirting

then
denying

cloud
calligraphy

Jadran Zalokar ::: Haiku & Image

on the gale -
green leaves
listen a sea

Haïku ::: Raffael de Gruttola
Image ::: Wilfred Croteau

Memorial Day
the music box ballerina
stops mid-melody

winter night
this dead
poet has
written
the same
poem as i

Woman, Dying

THE WISH TO DIE AND THE WILL to live, her eyes beseeching me to wet her lips, her lips when wet beseeching me to 'slip her something to be out of it all quick.'

These women, with their long, fighting deaths, gritting their toothless gums as a new morning forces itself in through the lattices of blinded wards, whiskery- chinned: they can teach a man something, something a man can't learn from a man.

Maybe it's their last pitiful act of mothering.

> as she lies dying
> I tell her the crocuses
> are early this year . . .

Del Doughty :::

Lingering Heat

THE LONG DRIVE BACK from the Indianapolis airport: it's dark outside, raining lightly, and the radio's playing, but I can hear little sobs and sighs from her side of the car. Her mother is dying. Leah cries all the way home, and this morning she is moody around the house. At breakfast she says there's a feeling of autumn in the air. I agree, but later the sun comes out strong and begins soaking up the puddles from last night's rain. I take the boys to the park to shoot hoops and run around. The wind blows hard, but it's a hot summer wind from the south and before long we're all tired and sweaty. Luke and Jack want to play on the old tank, so I walk over and watch while they clamber up and down the armored sides.

> lingering heat
> I rest in the shade of the tank
> at Memorial Park

::: Jamie Edgecombe

Shodo

Scribbling through the badly brushed characters with the wrong stroke order, they suddenly become beautiful, veiled and somehow resemble a dragon. The pretense of delicate kanji, luckily penned by the hand of this novice, evolves into sincerity. I will stamp my hanko in the opposite bottom corner, frame it with a deep blue border, hang it on the wall and never understand its power over me.

> Gleaming black
> The scent of autumn pavements
> Fills everything

And it is strange, where our minds drift to while wondering through music and the movement of brushes. Taking a large one-meter by one-meter piece of fine paper, slightly see-through and incredibly absorbent, I dip my brush in time to my *shodo* rhythm and then into the dark watery ink. Prizing away the excess, I dart a glance out of the window and catch an eye full of Hokkaido's glorious autumn colors, which remind me of a photograph I once saw or a haibun I once read about New England and start thinking how it would be nice to go there and in words I am home. Home. English soil: the chipped, shattered, weathered and worn mix of debris and biological cells: ink into paper: *tomaru*: quick stroke: *tomaru*, stroke, stroke: *tomaru*: draw.

A signpost
Labeling this place as Plymouth
when it isn't at all

As I approach a difficult kanji, deciding how to scale it against the other characters and spaces of the page, the world turns white and black, one-meter by one-meter square and Japan relaxes into the sound of a brush streaking paper.

Work, Labor, Play

I NEVER THOUGHT OF WHAT MY FATHER DID as "work". That was done by those we collectively called "the men". They were, to use my father's phrase, "laborers". They dug nursery stock, bound each shrub in burlap, loaded trucks, planted trees; watered, hauled, and sweated. Each year I became more self-conscious of the uselessness of my books, and games and plays. I invented acts in the enormous freedom of afternoons while "men worked".

That odd look an outsider, an idler, always has around those working, those with authority to be truly still.

Although my childhood was probably typically middle class, I was paralyzed with guilt and self-disgust, in first inklings of class war, caught in reading and watching B-movies like *Anastasia*, I recognized myself in Marie Antoinette and the last of the Romanovs.

That fall I worked for him and didn't go back to school. I hauled railroad ties and timbers, boots soaked in creosote; laid brick, Dutch block, sprayed water through candles of pines until the red clay bled through burlap; always fretting and threshing words, repeating lines of Keats' *Ode to Autumn* until I'd taste the syllables; September, the milky sweat of rhubarb and rye grass; October, the walnut blue shellac, the flayed red leaves of sumac, into November, carving sod like dirty glass from frozen pallets ...

September morning
green hay steams
against my chest

Marcia Fairbanks :::

Not Yet Spring

SOFT FLAKES MAKE A WHITE COVERLET on overwintered leaves and needles. That particular tree appears as a happenstance of thin forked trunk and bare limbs. The woman is not looking at the tree. She sees a docile yard and house amid a cluster of small, tidy homes in a secure, rural community of aging people. A branch of that tree brushes a dusting of snow from her head as she follows the realtor to the front door. This is where she will spend her widowhood. After sixty years with the same man.

Mother's Day

The tree has already leafed, a deep magenta accent against the yellow siding of her new house, when her daughter comes from far away to help with the moving. They arrange her furnishings just as they had been in the old house, even down to placement of the paintings, pillows, photographs, cranberry glass inside the hutch and German steins on top. This reassures both women. Containers of tansy, lavender and lemon balm, liberated from the old garden, rest against the tree's trunk.

Their Anniversary Month

She looks out the window beyond her computer screen through the burnished leaves of the Japanese maple tree. A pleasing contrast to the green of raked lawn, tall oaks, and sighing pines. She has learned to do research on the Internet. *Acer palmatum*, botanical name comes from its leaf, which has five or more deep lobes and resembles a human hand. The tree's nursery nametag has disintegrated. She chooses a name for it from among the 100 cultivated varieties of Japanese maple. *Bloodgood*. She imagines her daughter and grandchildren smiling at her whimsy.

After the First Frost

The leaves of Bloodgood are transmuted now to brilliant red, festive as a giant Christmas poinsettia. Her tree has thrived in the dappled shade. It will become, with maturity, a rounded silhouette, wider than its height. These traits—roundness and the need for protection from harsh light—they share. The thought engages her imagination. She knows her tree will continue to mark the seasons. She plans to be around, to notice its clusters of purple flowers. Rake up its winged seedpods. Brush wet snow off its bare branches when winter comes.

> samara—winged fruit
> spiral down when blossoms pass,
> meet the turning earth

Donna Fleischer :::

Petersen Field

LATE WINTER BONE STILLNESS of the field. dog's soft footfall herding
gait in figure eights encircling us, ghost-like, chasing shadows
as they engulf us; knows no less than we whose footsteps spoon
snow parfait crust halted by a clutch of briar on the northside of
the workers' house "in ruin before they left ten years ago, " says
this new friend and suddenly we're in the open field—escaped
into late day light and free, for a while, to feel the farm's pass-
ing millennium; the golf course recently finalized that will come
of the next. we turn slowly to face each other. staggering grey-
ness of sky surprises with a hem of orange light from behind the
far away and darkening hills

> the white dog
> up the snowy rise
> disappears

Kaikoura

AT THE SEA'S EDGE, I estimate compass setting, point out from the rocks, push- mower roll one hand out from my heart toward tomorrow. In the grammatic space inhabited by my brother, I make him a thumb winged plane, palm down, further and further out there. In reply he zig- zags a tutorial pointer across a map in the air. A map on which I see him already gone, barely arrived. Six years since last we met.

We cross the broken scripted rocks: geological glyphs smoothed and pooled by the tide. Surf washed, wave worn inlets are littoral character traits in the script. I wave for his attention. He responds shrugging eyebrows and shoulders. I scoop bracket-fulls of air before me to my chest, sample a scoop at my lips and splay fingers from my mouth with gastronomic gusto, and a Latin pout. Pensive eyebrows raised, he nods.

> the rocks text
> & deaf sign—shell spirals
> hear the sea

Over rocks patchy with seaweed, we find ways out to separate stone jottings for a view south around the headland.

Pointing northeast, right past him, I turn his attention to a couple with jeans rolled up, wading ashore through the incoming tide, from sea locked rocks. He zooms in with his video camera, points his diary. I see the rerun on television that night.

          no seals in sight
          the back of a black rock
          raises its head

Months later I receive his video of the world: takeoffs, landings,
train rides, bus rides, the sights captured by a memory truer
than mine.

::: Jen Hawkins

Untitled

I WITHSTOOD A DIFFICULT PREGNANCY. Consented to an adoption. I did not prepare to miss the boy. Did I expect a cloud? Some generic cherub? How did a body conceive what a mind could not fathom? His earlobes, his eyelids, were specific, intricate. I knew him. His voice stuck in me like the sea in a shell. I relinquished a baby, and took on a burning sort of transience.

> falling star—
> wishing you were
> here to see it

There is no explanation for giving him up. I cannot defend a miracle, cannot glorify resignation. The adoption was finalized, but not the conflict. Everyone was some mother's child, and I could not bear it. Bear this ghost- cord pulled taut at three- hundred miles.

> dandelion scatter—
> halo
> on a long wick

Time passes, as does my longing. Springtime, nightfall, the crook of my arm; these are no longer evidence of loss. The baby grows fat—he outgrows the months and spaces I made hollow. And he fits against his new mother as if he grew there.

> north-side moss—
> the baby
> at her breast

Elizabeth Hazen :::

Shadows Cross

I LEAVE THE TRAIL AND CLIMB to a mossy outcrop not far away. From here I can watch the woods. A three-inch millipede passes. Another. Another. Eleven.

> a thousand feet
> above sea level
> wild columbine

Below me a red fox trots along the trail I just left. Scarcely a minute later a man and dog go the opposite way, walking in the very footprints.

> empty snake skin
> the tips of ferns
> still curled

Nothing happens. Dog and man miss the fox. Dog and man and fox miss me. The millipedes miss each other and the rest of us. Perhaps we are all on different planes.

> trail of birch pollen
> bird shadows cross
> each other

temple yard
the sound
of stone buddhas

A. C. Missias ::: Haiku & Image

new grave —
the trampled grass
already recovering

rockfall
the trail guide
clears his throat

Bruce Ross ::: Haiku & Image

overnight snow
the small rounded mound
of stone Buddha

::: Doris Heitmeyer

Blackout

THE DREAM IS SO FAMILIAR I must have had it before. Walking home at 3 a.m., I don't see another soul on the streets. On empty avenues, traffic lights flash green, yellow, red. Then ahead of me the lights begin going out. I have not experienced such a blackout in twenty years. I leave the lighted area and enter the dark streets ahead. Tall buildings loom on either side; I sense rather than see them, a denser black closing in on a canyon of darkness. I feel on the brink of some adventure, like a child trespassing where it has been told not to go.

Waking, I realize I have again forgotten to look for the stars.

the hour before dawn:
black snowflakes
from a red sky

William J. Higginson :::

Santa Fe Shopping Carts

THE BRAND- NEW STORE COMES with brand- new shopping carts, and in the first few weeks when there is lots of help around and people are impressed with the new carts, there are few casualties. However, as the first month or so passes, one or another suffers a bent caster housing and a wheel that has its own direction in mind. Other carts develop flat- sided wheels; pushing one of them is like moving crosswise over a dirt road. Finally, a wheel breaks off altogether, leaving a gleaming axle that soon picks up stray mop strands.

Such carts gradually congregate—usually at the back of the in- store cart corral. Near the end of a long day they are often the only carts left in the store, the personnel situation having deteriorated along with the condition of the carts. A few stragglers, hardier than their shut- in cohorts, staunchly defend their rights to various choice car- parking spaces. They're not about to move on without a lot of coaxing.

The occasional cart, borrowed temporarily to wheel the groceries to a tracthouse, ends up in a nearby arroyo, where its baby seat becomes the base for a birds- nest. When the monsoon season hits, mid summer, the cart sinks into the silt and catches debris, thus ensuring its permanent place in the landscape.

> summer storm
> a shopping cart rolls past
> the end of the lot

Sometimes a cart is trundled off in its prime by a human who employs it to carry all worldly possessions. Such a cart may be seen shining through the dusty leaves of a small grove of Russian olive trees, or gleaming dully where the river has gone dry in the shade under a bridge.

> socks hang
> air crisp through the chrome
> of the shopping cart

Even this lucky cart, however, serves only its allotted time. Come winter, the homeless person sleeps in the library during the day, keeping on the move at night, or possibly signing in at a shelter for a night out of the gritty wind.

By early spring, it is time for a shipment of new shopping carts.

> deep in the arroyo
> just the red handle
> of a shopping cart

Ken Jones :::

The Inlet

AT LAST A THICKENING LINE between sea and sky. To starboard a thin green spit sharpens and lengthens on the ebb tide. With sails furled we putter up the winding creek, through mud and marsh. A scuttle of shrill oystercatchers works the tideline. At the tiller, I follow the waymarks of ancient mariners.

> Crooked withies
> feet in shallows
> gesture skywards

We drop anchor where the creek broadens out. The motor falls silent in a solitude which is neither land nor sea. The only object on this inland water is a ruined boathouse breaking the line of brown and green shoreline some five hundred yards away. We lower our "pram"—a tiny dinghy. One rows with short, cramped strokes against a freshening wind, back to back with the other kneeling in the bow. Both yacht and boathouse seem distant now, in this threatening expanse of dark, choppy water.

> Hunched in the pram
> shallow or not
> a bottomless depth

We beach on a drift of sand, and scramble up the grassy dyke. But nothing connects the boathouse to anywhere else. There is nowhere else. Veined with muddy creeks, the marshland stretches away into the haze. We take our fill—the lap of water, harsh cries of birds, and the little salty, leathery plants that live between the tides. I take a rusty baler to the boathouse boat.

Clinker built
through broken ribs
the dry sand drifts

Back across the sound the yacht towers above us. "Jump!" Together from the pram, lest one capsize the other. We decide to wait until the moon refills the haven. Idle, sunny hours. I nod off, and my water stained copy of Erskine Childers' *Riddle of the Sands*—an inshore yachtsman's mystery read—falls on the cabin floor.

Cries of curlews
all day long we swing
at our moorings

Back down the creek towards the open sea, running before a fresh evening breeze. Beneath a starlit sky we show our navigation lights.

Cradle of dreams
rocked by the wind
drawn by the tides

Ken Jones :::

The Long Wait

The Waiting Room
where time waits
on the sluggish clock

WE WHO ARE ADMITTED EACH MORNING are in fact the fortunate ones. A 1960s building gone to seed. Green linoleum worn through to the outlines of strange and unfamiliar continents. Visceral foam rubber protrudes through the slashes in the upholstered benches. Always the same smell of stale tobacco, disinfectant and urine from the broken lavatory. Faded notices warn of the penalties of giving information which you know to be false. The only animation comes from a limping ceiling fan. It lurches and wheezes round and round, flicking pale sunlight across the room. And there is one long grimy window—

High flat roof
littered with things
broken, forgotten and unseen

We are a furtive, shabby crowd of men. People come in through a left hand door, and the room is always full.

Thin yellow finger
the fag end stubbed
and stubbed again

In this room everything waits, and has grown old and tired with the waiting. There is nothing other than waiting. See that one, how he listlessly reaches for a dog-eared magazine.

> "World's Most Beautiful Women"
> flicked through
> and cast aside

Once in a while a white coated official comes in through the right hand door ("Authorised Personnel Only") . Armed with a clipboard, he calls a surname, nailing one or two forenames to it.

> The pity of names
> typed, listed, ticked,
> and shouted out

Sometimes no one responds. At other times the fortunate—or unfortunate—person gets up and is conducted through the door. I don't know who is successful and who isn't. You just don't see them again.

I've been coming here now for more weeks than I can remember. And I must confess to a perverse fondness for the place. Yesterday I think I detected a wry smile play briefly on the lips of another of the regulars. To tell you the truth, I have forgotten what I'm waiting for. I suppose that can happen if you wait long enough. Anyway, it's always someone else they call. And yet—

> Dread time
> my name at last
> but sounding
> like someone else's

Jim Kacian :::

The Interview

WHAT JOY! in his voice, explaining, explaining: the way is clearly marked, but the following of it is hard, requires discipline, striving, concentration, requires the moving through, the working out, the awareness of—Nothing! and that realized it is easy, easy, the path is broad and there is nowhere we can fall through, or away, or off . . .

> on an interview tape
> from far away
> the song of foreign birds

::: Jim Kacian

Pet Name

SHE GOT HER, GOOFY, just out of high school:
a pure-bred baby, all slobber and spunk,
a one-woman dog for a one-dog woman.
Scared silly with owning, she named her Boo—

short for Boofer, a comic book buddy
extravagant beyond her small-town means:
a questioning tail, big hair and black tongue,
cold eyes large as her nancy drew dreams.

Married the only boy she'd ever known,
moved to the city, then the city beyond.
Traded husband for lover, a boss for a partner,
a loft for a condo, Peekskill for Provence.

Through the dog days of her dog years
she was the genius of a portable hope,
the locus of their ever-yawing walk
'til, tired, she wandered once away . . .

Not surprised, at her eulogy, to learn she was psychic,
felt the pain of her mistress days before her,
sat in with the board, ate cookies from the table
—surprised not by the tale but only the telling

to find that her name, through all the years
had remained as it was, immutable Boo,
short, now we are told, for Kabuki,
an elegant and exotic form of theatre.

comes up with the shovel
while digging the grave—
heartleaf*

* the elegant and exotic name for wild ginger

::: Jim Kacian

twilight and

I am waiting for him in the kayak. I'm reading a small book of
poetry I have brought with me, not watching, but alert. When he
comes, I hear the soft plink of him breaking the surface,
unmistakable as a bird call. He sees me immediately, of course,
and signals to his mate, still in the lodge, with a call like the first
four notes of *Für Elise*: a falling semitone, then repeated,
rasped as though played on a kazoo. She chucks a couple of
times, and I never do see her. He disappears, and I turn the boat
around and wait, and 30, 40 seconds later, he pops up, turning
the dusklight into a series of small waves which flow toward me,
bearing light, and pass right through me on into the darkening
east.

> I am the center
> of the perfect circle
> the beaver swims

Jim Kacian :::

wilderness

SIXTH DAY ON THE TRAIL. Smoke from five fires has sealed the pores of my skin. Sweat from five hikes has filled the hollows and creases of my body. Scent from five nights wrapped against the elements has filled my clothes.

I like it.

> sixth day
> the sharp aroma
> of wild meat

The Edge of House Lights

THE BUSINESS OF THE LONG DAY has settled; homework's started; the clang of the dishes, too, has quieted as the sun divides its embers among the dark boughs of sumac and pine.

> to the world as it is
> the morning glory has closed
> its white petals

Our family dog and I take a walk. Adopted last spring and by then already four, what he steals in disobedience he more than replaces with affection. The devotion of dogs and families has no exact parallel, and over time, feelings learn to slip wordlessly between long floppy ears and the palms of our hands. I've come to relish these nightly walks.

> children
> how their laughter trickles
> into autumn twilight

About half way along our return loop, he halts abruptly, watching over the darkening field like a statue until a burst of whiteness, strangely disembodied as if exploding out of nothing, rivets us both to its movement. Straining to focus, I can see the brown hide of an adult deer just preparing to leap over the pasture fence. Then with a powerful vault of remarkable lightness and grace, it clears the fence as effortlessly as a bird.

We resume our walk until I notice a stirring in the field again, and drawing closer, I find there is a second deer, much smaller and thin, which is trying to follow the other but cannot quite make the jump. We stop a safe distance away so as not to make its task any more difficult.

After two more attempts fail, the young deer pauses. Into the muscles of its spindly legs it drives its courage, for it runs back nearly three times as far to gain a longer running start. Almost soundlessly and with a long arching stride, it joins the other across the road, the two white lanterns vanishing together into the moonless dark

> the night fields
> a stillness made rounder
> without crickets

Advancing deeper into the woods, their footsteps soon become slow and leisurely, now free of headlights (and men and dogs) . In the night's windless quiet, the leaves beneath their hooves mark their increasing distance with a crisp, brittle sharpness, and I listen until a cold silence erases them altogether.

> on the edge of house-lights
> another world is dawning
> in the scent of wet leaves

Haïku ::: Ryokan

Image ::: Ron Moss

the thief left it behind —
the moon
at the window

ryokan.

Angelee Deodhar ::: Haiku & Image

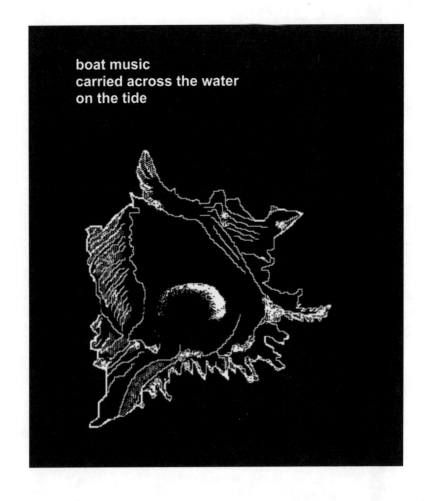

boat music
carried across the water
on the tide

Haiku & Image ::: Pamela Miller Ness

sitting zazen
the hole
in Buddha's heel

Not able to fall asleep The owl on its part, I on mine, Not able to fall asleep The owl on its part, I on mine,

ふくろうはふくろうでわたしはわたしでねむれない

::: Robin Lovell

A Cormorant

AMBLING AROUND THE SHADY LAGOON during the last days of summer among moored yachts I espy a cormorant feeding, its dives following a casual rhythm. I await its surfacing, each time delighted to see its head ripple the water. Gently the moored boats rock, their rigging clangs. The lagoon leads into open waters and, about a kilometer off shore, a group of sail boats tack towards a starting buoy. Among whitecaps their sails fashion the wind into curves and arcs as they sweep in and out of each other's paths seeking the best position. Behind me I hear the cormorant dive.

> starting gun sounds
> waiting for the cormorant
> to surface again

Catherine Mair :::

Towards Her Wedding Day

DROPPING DOWN FROM LAKE TAUPO and the volcanic plateau the road
risks its way through shades of violet and umber tussock land,
deeper into dark, forested ravines.

> mist clinging to ridges
> veiling great Rimu, Totara
> and Kahikatea trees

I imagine Katie driving the lonely miles in her 1981 Cortina, her
champagne- coloured, silk wedding dress spread across the
back seat. She comes bearing gifts—small boxes with two heart-
shaped chocolates in each, and tied with fine green ribbon, for
every guest. She has handcrafted the cream, beeswax candles
for each table.

> one passenger
> her black, curly coated dog
> tuned to Katie

The aloneness deepens in intensity, where that particular green,
which is the New Zealand bush, presses close by, and above the
road. In places it would be easy to let go and hurtle from the road,
where it twists around precipitous corners, and plummet into
one of the gun- metal, grey rivers.

                              forest-green service
                              booklets, packed in a shoebox
                              safe in the boot

Katie knows the patches on this road, over the ranges, where the
black ice takes control of tyres, and spins cars over the brink into
a vortex of air and the crunch of rock.

                              Sasha presses closer
                              to Katie's leg—it's barely
                              Springtime

Ed Markowski :::

Soft Hands

I TOOK CARE OF HIM FOR THREE NIGHTS prior to his surgery. He was a wiry old man with thin white hair and a nose "That was made by taking about a thousand punches of the sort boxers don't remember nor ever gets paid for", he said in a voice "That come up gradual from drinking too damned much whiskey to kill off the pain". He sure was a talker.

"Born and raised on a hog farm down in North Carolina. Learned to barbecue a whole pig by the time I was six year old. Started boxing at twelve. 1935. Two hour later, I knocked down a boy twice my size in a three round match. Five year past that, I won the welterweight division at the Atlanta Golden Gloves. Thought I was gonna be the next Joe Louis, till the war blowed in.

"Did three years in the South Pacific, come out with a purple heart, married, and boxed my way around the Gulf, from Biloxi to New Orleans till Virginia got tired of patching me up and seeing me drunk.

"Moved up here in 1956 and did pretty good at the car factory. Raised our kids, and put 'em all through college. Virginia and me been married fifty- three year now."

I was giving the old boxer his medications when the doctor came in to explain the procedure to him and his family. "Piece of cake" the doctor said. "A champ like you will be up and about in no time."

"Look here doc, " he said, "The war ain't killed me. Boxing ain't killed me. Whiskey ain't killed me. Five kids ain't killed me. And fifty-three year with the same woman ain't killed me." He smiled, made a fist, and shook it at the doctor. "I sure ain't afraid of no man with soft hands and a little bitty knife."

The next night room 304 was empty. In report the nursing supervisor said, "Henry Leonard coded after surgery. Pulmonary embolism." She's not much of a talker.

after his surgery
a wrinkled snapshot
the family left behind

Michael McClintock :::

Once in a Meadow, Near Los Osos

God of Abraham, Isaac, and Jacob, the One who with a single thought filled the universe, God of the Exodus and the empty tomb:

IN THE YEAR THE SNOWS CAME LATE and the coastal ranges alone made room for spring, many times dandelions delayed my journey, their faces all innocent, clean, wholesome—they called me off the road, they unraveled my purpose like a spool and threw away my coat, crowding in upon me, they and the daisies and the poppies—most especially the poppies, fields of them, in riot and aflame, wanton and loving with color.

My heart was rampant and willing and so into their beds I went radiant and sprawled naked among them, embraced and kissed, flaring like a candle.

God forgive me what was done among the dandelions, the wildflowers, most especially the poppies.

a poppy . . .
a field of poppies!
the hills blowing with poppies!

Unnatural Amber

1

> all day in spring,
> deer cross the high meadow
> into the clouds

I CAME DOWN FROM MY TINY WRITING CABIN in the mountains to accompany my friend George to the annual "Battle of the Robots" event at a small park in downtown Los Angeles. The place was surrounded by skyscrapers and next to a massive old cathedral. George, who teaches engineering and applied physics at the California Institute of Technology, lures me to the spectacle each spring. The contest engages the minds of students who are likely someday to see Jupiter rise over the frozen oceans of Europa, or to examine strange, broken, wall- like formations far back in some Martian canyon of the Nirgal Vallis rift.

But now, here, they create and fight small robot monstrosities intended to stop, dismember, and destroy other small robot monstrosities, the combat taking place within an area the size and shape of a boxing ring.

"Don't pull that poetic sensitivity crap with me, " George says. "You know it fascinates you, but you don't know enough about it to be a pessimist. Each year you try to figure it out, but can't. Your poetic knowledge of the world shudders at the thought of raw conflict. What use is your poetry in this context?"

"Shut the hell up, George."

But he had a point. I thought gloomily of a poem I had written a few weeks back, on a tangent theme:

a shining world—
dew drops for the duckling
and the beetle it eats

I'd shown George that poem.

2

We took our seats on high bleachers and watched the mechanical slaughter through opera glasses.

All of the combatant machines appeared to be based on insectoid models, except one. The exception was a beautiful, gleaming white sphere, about eighteen inches in diameter. I searched through the printed program and found its description. It was named "Amber" and had been made by a team of paleontology, engineering and chemistry students. Its combat strategy was purely defensive and non-violent—simply to sit there and do nothing unless attacked. When touched or jostled by an attacker, Amber's designed response was literally to expectorate glue. Chemically, the glue was approximately that of natural amber—the kind paleontologists love to collect and inspect for the twenty-million-year-old bugs preserved within it. The stuff inside Amber, held in a reservoir, dried to hardness in a few seconds upon exposure to the air. A gyroscope mechanism and a few balanced weights within the sphere controlled the ball's movements; simple sound and motion sensors on the outer surface determined when and in what direction the goo would be expelled from a top-mounted spigot onto an adversary.

"Brilliant," I said, reading the program's description. "It intends to glue its enemies to the floor, or to muck up the moving parts of their weapons!"

George fluttered his eyelids and sneered. "The idea's asinine, " he said. "Pacifist philosophy does not translate into the natural world, or into physics."

In the first of five elimination rounds, Amber did well by gluing fast to the floor a mean-looking mechanical grasshopper with ice-pick mandibles. The thing had leapt onto Amber's smooth surface, failed to get a grip, and fell off to its doom. It twitched just a few moments before becoming immobile in a glob of the maple-colored, unnatural amber. By winning just that one round, Amber went from one of thirty-two battling robots to one of sixteen.

"Pure luck, " said George. The man was clearly surprised.

3

> city towers
> brighten and dim
> a gusting wind

The remaining sixteen paired off for the second round. Amber drew a match with a flat, segmented, worm-like device that destroyed its victims by getting under them, then flexing and flipping them over onto their backs. George scowled as we watched Amber handle that little horror with ease, gluing its head to the floor in seconds after the beast's first onslaught: it had no way at all of upsetting a sphere.

Amber was suddenly one of eight finalists. I could see alarm on George's face. His confident world was getting a shake and a goose-feather up the nose.

4

> new ones appear
> as others pass—
> spring clouds

A light rain fell as the third round began. Amber was paired off against a monster whose one weapon was a buzz saw on a flexible proboscis- like appendage coming out of the center of a turtle- like body. The monster shot across the floor and cut through Amber like a melon. It was over in seconds—but for both of them. Amber died in a fountain of its own fluid, which likewise gushed over the monster turtle, puddling it and affixing it firmly to the floor. Officially, the contest between the two was a draw; of course, neither machine went on to the next round.

"What did I tell you?" George said, blinking at me. I thought he looked like a turtle at that moment. The rain had ceased; it was sunny again.

"Wait until next year, you gas bag, " I said. "A few tweaks, and Amber is going to give you a new lesson in physics, pal. It already has. Do the math."

And of course he knew I was right. Just the concept alone had defeated three- quarters of the field that day. Poetic sensitivity, indeed.

>   the hiss
>   of a broom
>   on wet cement

Finegand Chain Three

FOUR HUNDRED HORSEPOWER of Mack Ultraliner reverses among half a dozen clones, queued to dock at the Works. Ray's face in the mirrors earlobes the cab, focused—intent. Perfectly aligned the trailer nudges into rubber buffers, the tractor unit remorselessly closes the gap, telescoping the tang, crashing together! Shiny steel capped boots tread the clutch and stomp—the brakes snort!

> *arbeit macht frei—*
> red raddled lambs balk
> partway down

Shepherds' dogs bark, steel tubed gates rise and swing, and fingers stab tallies into the air. Lambs leap imagined chasms. Blue raddled between their ears—the mob steams, huddled in the pen's rear third. Ewes squat and gush urine, handfuls of Hooker's Green beads roll through gaps in steel meshed grating. Not one of Andy's numbers was struck the other night. He pulls out the Lotto chit, gives it one more inspection; then it's screwed up and falling—

> above Crete—
> the paratrooper shudders,
> raining blood

Ali nods repeatedly toward the kiblah marked on the wall, *"Bi-smi llahi l-rahmani l-rahimi"* he mumbles when the Iranian mullah visits. Later the red hatted boardwalker switches on the speaker. Humming to decanted Led Zeppelin and snagging hocks, he watches Ahmed's whites speckle with crimson—

early Sunday—
beercan rolls on
the Stirling straight

Len's knife strokes the carcass along the pizzle line, his wrist tilting the blade from thumbs up and over, sliding the point in, twisting it quarter of a turn and down. The guts billow out against his lower forearm. He slashes left and right, scabbards the knife and with both hands reaches in and wrenches down, then up and out, pivoting around to drop the pluck on the gut tray. He could do it blindfolded.

"Easy as, like bloody magic mate".

That accent, Birmingham?

sudden peripheral movement—
in Belfast flinching, cocking the FN
automatically

Inch

TOUGH WEEK AT WORK, incessant rain in the city too, suburban acres of lawn to be cut. The crew pent up in the van, scratchy as a bag of weasels. But on Thursday the sun shines, and it's pay-day, for me at least. For them it's a 25-quid top-up on a meagre disability allowance.

Between mowings, a chance to spend a moment with A, try to find him inside that black cloud. Inch, his few intimates call him when they're feeling fond, and he'll grin wolfishly, and they'll insult each other with warmth and wit, the rueful alliance of the oppressed with the taunted, bolstered by withering contempt for the mongos, pigs and suits who people their world of not-us. In the open prison of his own life he's an old lag doing hard time. He's seen the counsellors and the programme devel-opers come and go like spring fashions, and met them coming round again.

See him raking leaves on a winter's day dressed in his jerkin with the broad hood shadowing his face, he's a medieval knave locked in the margins of a *Book of Hours*. Sit level with him on the bench and glance at his absorbed expression as he listens to vintage reggae—he's out there, burnin' babylon.

We sit on the kerb in the nuns' garden. The brief heat draws earthy odours from the leaf-mulch we spread in the rain last week.

There is little can be said. For that reason each word seems weighted. Between them he picks up pebbles from the path and

flicks randomly. I notice weeds, catch my mind flickering away
to plans for spraying, bring it back. He's talking about drawing,
that he'd like to draw. I know this. Does he draw? No, can't find
the right paper—rough paper. I suggest a shop. Maybe.

a pine seedling:
plucking it without thinking
sadness pours out

::: Fay O'Neill

A Journey to the Outback

CROSSING COUNTLESS MILES OF DRY LANDS and desert plains we travel ever westward. I say miles, because the only change here is the seasons, and 'kilometres' is one of those words that fits neither the feeling of eternal time nor the immense landscape. We come to crests of hills where space too great to be measured reaches out to a rim where the earth's surface seemingly meets the sky.

> horizons—
> hazy limits
> of vision

Gradually without realising, the distraction of modern suburban life, and the absence of noise that accompanies it, fades from our minds. The further we travel the isolation forces us to look with appreciation at the inner beauty of this great outback.

Gaps between boulders frame a picture of a vast wilderness of rolling hills and valleys. Clouds form a moving mosaic of dark shadows and textures on the red earth as waves of heat shimmer and dance across the plains. Over this arena desert breezes whisk and dry soil into spirals of ghostly dancers

> dust—
> whipped into whirlwinds
> vanishes in puffs

Leaving the safely of our vehicle we trek over this wide land and marvel at its incredible age, at the same time experiencing a powerful intangible feeling of an indomitable spirit watching and waiting with a quiet endless patience.

The highlight of our day is making camp early in the evening and watching the glorious sunset paint clouds the colour of blood before turning to hues of soft greys, bright pinks and finally beautiful blues rimmed with gold. It is a time of exodus when animal and bird life sensing the end of daylight seek the shelter and safety of their nightly abodes.

> sunset—
> in perfect 'v' formation
> birds wing home

After these natural wonders, of colour abundance and boisterous energy, an eerie feeling of stillness and complete isolation steals over the land then with the unhurriedness of the outback night slowly envelopes us in a black silky curtain.

> twilight—
> melding shadows thickening
> nightfall

Our fire casts a mellow glow and dimly illuminates the rocky outcrops beside our camp. It occurs to me the vastness of the outback has been shut out and we are safely cocooned within this circle of golden light in an aura of peace.

> flames—
> silhouette figures
> around campfire

We talk on into the night, happy to sit and enjoy each other's company and breathe in the cool scent of clear fresh air. Occasionally, across the diamond studded sky a star flashes, crashing through the velvety darkness like a silver arrow. We make a wish.

Haiku ::: Elizabeth Howard
Image ::: Jennifer Quillen

midday sun
iridescent dragonfly
loops over the lake

not yet
touching —

not yet spring

Haiku ::: Dakotsu
Image ::: Kuniharu Shimizu

breaking off a silver grass -
unexpected heaviness
of the plant

をりとりてはらりとおもきすすきかな

Raffael de Gruttola ::: Haiku
Wilfred Croteau ::: Image

spring thaw   a sparrow
    alone   on thin ice

blink

BILL TELLS THE STORY of his stroke on Super Bowl Sunday. A base-ball player, golfer and high school honor student. Much of that taken away as he sat in a recliner during halftime. He is a new advisee of mine at the College. Six years, and only a sophomore. He takes one course at a time. One day at a time, he laughs. Dark glasses. A white cane. He finds the buildings on campus by the colors and shapes of air conditioning units on top. Recently, they repainted our building a different color, throwing off his inter-nal map. He found his way by the different scents of flowers and shrubs bordering the sidewalks. "You turn left at the roses, then right at the mock orange. It's easy."

I saw Bill only a few more times. We chatted about the new plants on campus.

humid stillness
in the bush
the frog's blink

Jo Pacsoo :::

Mountain Reflections

THE BUS DRIVES AWAY leaving darkness. I stumble down the rough drive until, turning a corner, lights, greetings. After supper the retreat begins in silence. The days have a pattern: meditate, walk, listen, question, discuss.

> sound of the gong
> lingers   early
> morning yawns

By the second afternoon backs begin to ache. Behind the Buddha rain and sunlight cross the mountain; rainbows shimmer in the mist; the farmer tends his sheep. We settle into stillness.

> in the silence
> intense irritation flips
> to affection

As the week moves on, assumptions are questioned. What do we know about time, space, ourselves and the world? Attitudes are shaken, common sense challenged. Feelings of outrage, of wanting to leave. We take comfort in food, walk down to the lake where rams with ripe testicles eye ewes across the fence. In the water mountain reflections shatter in ripples.

Something shifts in my solid world view. Earnestness cracks into laughter.

The trains are disrupted by engineering works so I leave
early, return up the drive in grey dawn

> clouds
> hide the mountain
> hum of morning chants

Jo Pacsoo :::

On Top of the World

DAWN. Sun touches the highest peaks as I set out to climb the crag above the town of Leh, Ladakh. Every day a monk offers early morning prayers in two small gompas (monasteries) on this hill. The path has been washed away in recent rain and the scree slides beneath me. I thread my way up to the lowest monastery.

> buildings blend with rock
> strings of coloured flags flutter
> against the sky

Usually a few tourists come to view the gompas at opening time but today I am the only one among a crowd of Ladakhis coming up the path from the other side. I ask a man if it is a special occasion.

"No", he replies. "Once every month we put up new prayer flags. On a day that is good, " he adds.

On the summit, in the ruins of a third gompa, a fire is lit, fed with butter and herbs. Long poles are embedded in the edge of the precipice.

> young men hang in air
> with bundles of bright flags
> new links cross the valley

Chanting begins. I hang back, fearing to intrude but a smiling woman takes my hand, draws me into the circle. We have no words in common; I sit beside her in silence as sound flows round us with smell of butter and fragrant smoke. Every now and then my neighbour throws rice into the air, stops for a chat or points out something in the town below, then turns the pages of her book to join the chants again. The script is in Tibetan but the page numbers are familiar. She is reading from page 24.

Sunshine moves over the plain. Below, the cramped town, a few fields, small patch on a desert landscape. Early morning chill; sun withdraws in a cloudy sky, the wind is sharp. The prayers reach page 43.

> voices
> rise in space
> surrounded by nameless snow peaks

The chanting ends, after 86 pages, with sudden joyful shouts. We all stand and tsampa (barley flour) is passed round. Throw up, someone says to me.

I throw the flour into the air to general laughter as it falls on the head of a nearby youth. He shakes it out of his hair. "Not yet. Watch me."

Everyone begins to sing. We raise our fistfuls of flour three times. No longer a stranger, I am part of this hilltop communion as we cast our flour on the wind. It rises in a fine cloud.

> flour blows where we
> can't go — towards mountains
> which guard Tibet

Joanna Preston :::

Dig dig

"You have to dig deep, to bury your daddy."
                                    Romany Gypsy saying

1. DADDY'S LITTLE

Fathers and daughters. Bounced on his knee. Perched on his shoulders. Best seat in the house. Best dad on the block. Keep the bat straight. Keep your eyes on the ball. Want an ice cream? Want to come with me? Pocket money. Mowing the lawns. Saturday morning polishing shoes.

> lunar eclipse—
> a halo of grey hair
> around dad's head

2. TIED IN NOTS

First detention. First boyfriend. First pimples. First bra. First Not with that boy! First Not in those clothes! Not on a school night. Not while I'm here. Not in that tone of voice. Not on your life. Not likely. Not ever. Not under my roof.

> school ball—
> dad's angry voice
> from the car

3. Grown

New year. New town. New job. New life. New love. New family. New baby. New choices. New problems. New answers. New grass on his grave.

> beachside holiday—
> wiping salt water
> off the photos

Joanna Preston :::

Shoulder Reconstruction

SHE IS HOME from the hospital—right arm strapped to her side and across her chest, immovable. The empty right sleeve of her shirt sways like a metronome, setting the tempo as she walks gingerly across the muddy lawn and up the steps to the house.

> home at last—
> greeting the dog
> wrong handed

Three times a day I have to undo the straps and carefully straighten her arm, easing it against the spasms of muscle cramp. Lurid paisley bruises cover her chest, and a tiny line of stitches march millipede fashion across her collarbone. For ten minutes, three times a day, she has to remain motionless:

> the third time
> today—
> that same cryptic crossword

Neither of us is ready for this role reversal. Not knowing where to look as I give her a sponge bath, trying to remain impersonal and unembarrassed as I soap her breasts, her nipples becoming erect in the cross draft from the door as I pat her dry . . . silly. I am the age she was when she gave birth to me.

> washing
> my mother's breasts—
> we both giggle

::: Pat Prime

At Guilin

SUNRISE OVER THE LI RIVER. Limestone hills lift straight up from the water. Terraces and dwellings glint in the mountains above Guilin.

From a dirt road we descend rocky steps to the river. The scent of wood fires and the slow smokeless burning of refuse greets us. Vendors line the road to the river selling souvenirs, live animals, herbal remedies and aphrodisiacs.

> chickens squawk
> a faint odour of shit
> hangs in the air

The Li flows over smooth pebbles down to the sea. It is one of the most important waterways in the region. A fleet of tourist boats shadow the quay, sunshine flares on the unusual lime-stone formations, then rises above the hills.

It is Sunday on the river. Fishermen tie their cormorant's throats to prevent them swallowing the fish before letting them dive, women wash their family's clothes along the banks, and naked children swim in the brown water. Water buffalo wait to cross the river.

Why do these sights cause us pain? It is the pain of comparing the simple life of these peasants with our own luxuries at home. These images—flashed with the sun on the river—will follow us.

After a day spent on the river boat we return to Guilin. The moon is almost full and old men beat drums and blow bugles to scare away the demons.

across the river
a match flares and dims
sunset

Haiku & Image ::: Pamela A. Babusci

again love
eludes me . . .
autumn of my life

Muriel Ford ::: Haiku & Image

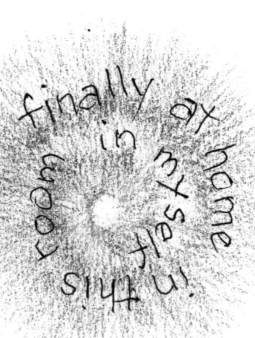

finally
in
this
room
myself
at
home
in

cloudburst —

a clown holding balloons

over his head

Karen Klein ::: Haiku & Image

returning home
starlings' wild chatter
from the ivy

Wasp

SUCH A STING—such a rapid swelling of the knuckle—so out of proportion with the wasp's thin-torsoed waist and dainty, thread-like feelers. One would think the smallest things should make the smallest pains, droplets of discomfort not lakes of torment. But not so. There seems to be a law that all agony grows of lesser things: the bubonic plague bacterium, the seed of jealousy, and the Hiroshima shell. The law's corollary is known well, that from great beginnings must come less or little. It's how to explain the Christian crusades, the master race, and our modern hope in artificial intelligence.

> wasps attacking
> from a mud hive—
> dumb, shrewd hate

Emily Romano :::

Saddle River Song

SMALLCAPS SUMMERTIME . . . I awaken to velvety darkness in a strange bed. In the night I've kicked back the sheet. Its white folds are faintly visible. I'm wide awake and feel miniscule in the vastnesses of the Saddle River countryside. I seem to be waiting for something . . .

> flooding the night
> a whippoorwill's song
> fills all hollows

Head-Smashed-In Buffalo Jump

FOR MORE THAN 10, 000 YEARS the Plains Indians stampeded herds of buffalo over cliffs to their deaths and butchered the animals for food beneath those cliffs. I live near the northern terminus of such jumps, Dry Island Buffalo Jump in Central Alberta. On several visits I pondered the beauty and starkness of the place that once served the hunter and gatherer aboriginals so well. In the heat of summer's end I was visiting one of the oldest and best preserved of these jumps. Head- Smashed-In Buffalo Jump southeast of Calgary. Despite the oppressive afternoon prairie heat I wandered down the dirt trail that passed beside the spot where the buffalo fell. A grasshopper moved over just a little in the dust as I walked past it. A young ivory moth chased its shadow into the weeds. A light but steady wind nestled the wild grasses. I paused at the killing ground but could not fathom the joy those hunters must have felt nor the cost of that joy. I looked up to the top of the cliff I had walked on earlier:

> Head-Smashed-In Buffalo Jump:
> orange gold lichen
> along the cliff's edge

Bruce Ross :::

Tulum

Tulum is the only Mayan temple site set on the ocean. The crumbling gray and black stone structures stand on a cliff above the crystal blue waters of the Caribbean. Visiting it again I find an indescribable beauty in these stones highlighted by the intense Yucatan sun and those blue waters. There is always an intense stillness here no matter how many tourists there are. Here again is a huge ancient iguana resting on the stone ruins as gray and black as it is. Once these uneven stones were stuccoed over and covered with red paint. In fact stucco painting was the most prevalent form of decoration at Tulum. When Juan de Grijalva sailed past it in 1518 he recorded that the buildings were all brightly colored like those back home in Seville.

> Tulum . . .
> the red hand prints faded now
> in afternoon light

::: Adelaide Shaw

Insomnia 3

Difficult to be thoughtless—free of thought—free of worries—
free of yesterday and tomorrow—free of that haiku forming from
somewhere behind my closed eyelids.

> the first bird call
> no longer waiting
> for sleep

Steve Sanfield :::

Looking Back on an Old Journey

IN THE AUTUMN OF 1988 I set out on a journey to Eastern Europe—
Poland, the Ukraine, East Germany. Ostensibly it was to do
background research for a book of stories I was writing about the
Fools of Chelm, the legendary numskulls of the Jewish oral
tradition. Though I had known these stories since childhood, I
needed a landscape to place them in. I needed to learn about the
trees and flowers, to experience sunrises and sunsets, to feel the
rain, to walk in the mud.

Recently, while looking through my notebooks, I was sur-
prised to discover that even though I filled scores of pages, I had
written only a few poems during my months' sojourn there. Why
so few is evident from those that did get recorded.

Road Kill

these seven geese
never white than now
soaked in their own blood

Sunday at Auschwitz

high school students hurrying
to finish their ice cream
before entering the crematorium

Dawn at Maijdanek

all these crows
on the white gravel
betray the official silence

Pines at Sobibor

this memorial grove
still twisted and stunted
forty years later

Flashback at Belzec

twilight
a distant train whistle
true terror

Kuniharu Shimizu :::

Holiday Haibun

A MOUNTAIN HAIJIN WENT TO THE SEA. I am at a hotspring spot along the coast of Japan Sea. (12 hour train ride from my town!) The hotspring is located in the open, right by the beach. A few steps away is the wide wide expanse of Japan Sea. I watch the huge sunset as I warm myself in the hotspring.

> calm sea . . .
> a string of wake
> leads to the setting sun

Basho, when he made the trip *Narrow Road of Oku*, walked along this area, wrote the following haiku:

> the rough sea—
> flowing toward Sado Isle
> the river of Heaven

Sado Isle is too far to see from where I am. And I do not stay outside to observe the river of Heaven, or the Milky Way. I have a party to attend that night. Having been in the hotspring to long, I am more attracted to cold beer and sake.

> a treat for travelers,
> milk for Basho
> and *sake* for me

::: John Stevenson

Spring

THERE IS NO FENCE or enclosing wall; no waste of space or undue
sentiment.

> country graveyard
> the close pass
> of a plow

John Stevenson :::

Untitled

with time
the piles of leaves
have settled

WHY DOES MY SON LIE to me about the trouble he's in? It's so much
like the trouble I was in.

deep in a dream
the door
to a storm cellar

Yellow

I REMEMBER ONCE when I was a little boy walking along a sidewalk in a quiet part of town. There was no one else around, no cars moving on the street and none, or few, parked along it. It was a bright, sunny morning in the summer. I came to a red fire hydrant and saw that the curbstone in front of it for about ten feet on either side had just been freshly painted a bright yellow. The paint glittered wetly. An open can was standing on the walk at one end of the painted stone. It was half full of the brilliant paint, and its top edge glimmered with wet paint that had dripped in yellow petals partway down the outside. A brush still yellow with paint was lying on the turned-over cover next to the can. The painter was nowhere to be seen. The silence was immense.

Somehow the sunshine of that day shone with and in that yellow paint with such a primal light that it still shines down through the years in my mind: the wet band of golden stone blazing coolly in the middle of a day of magic sunshine—and the yellow can blooming at one end of it like a great golden flower.

> a field of buttercups
> in the stillness of noon
> the sound of a brook

David Walker :::

Apart Together

still waters—
in perfect time
a wild goose dips

Apart—together, that's the way it is, the way that has evolved between us. We walk upon a mountain, The Black Mountain, *Mynydd Du*. Some thirty metres apart, he strides forth, confident, follow my leader. Without conversation, there is time to grow in the quiet rhythm of the walk, a sense of openness, receiving, making connections, sifting moments, the 'inside out' and the 'outside in'.

Apart is the way it began, at his birth, so vulnerable in my arms. Then, those special years together, the magical fantasy world of childhood, supporting, extending through the teens, till after University he stands, head and shoulders above me, his own person.

We strike out on a well-worn track, "The Coffin Route", snaking above the *Afon Sawdde* Valley, leaving a patchwork of tiny fields and homesteads that lighten and darken in the scudding clouds.

a pair of collies
work the flock
to a patch of sun

Generations before, these small communities gave up their menfolk to labour, sweat and toil in the mines and quarries of

South Wales. Many gave their lives.

   Mist seethes, shredded on stunted thorn, sheep dogs, muffled bitter fruit, lollop in the gusting wind below the summit of Fan Brycheiniog, coffin bearers from a craggy cowl sheltering the trundled gambo- cart, all hands to the iron rim that slips, sparks and chatters in the shale, lashed broken bundle laid square, brothers, workmates, pony sweat the 'Staircase' to bring him home one last time, his Mother waits, the women wait, on a bleak mountain track to *Llanddeusant* they rest ... their blue flecked pallor of the early bath, released from endless night to walk, the long walk ... the silent walk ... and later talk, the long talk unwrapping memories, telling and retelling tales punctuated by the cough, till tribal masks are riven by deep harmonies that drift upon the wind ... *Cwm Rhondda*, from the bowels of the earth ... together, one body, mind and spirit, 'they pilgrim through this barren land.'

> ragged grey clouds
> feathering the scarp
> the buzzards hang

Hooded now, leaning into the wind, we walk the edge of a vast abyss, the precipitous old red sandstone escarpment of *Bannaue Sir Gaer*. Mist boils over the rim from the cauldron far below, the glacial lake of *Llyn y Fan Fach*. Relentless, the wind skins raw the barren, savage flanks, purple and pink, drained from the summit now wreathed in grey mist. The weather is closing in— The distance between us shortens. Did I quicken my pace? Did my son shorten his stride? Without words, we fall in step together, it is time to tread these tracks with care. We make for the windbreak, a drystone walled enclosure that affords some protection. A desolate place to lodge when there is only the smell of sheep for company. 'Time for a cuppa.

Unplugging the special plastic mouthpiece, he sips still water from his sports bottle and unfolds the map. Tracing alternative tracks, his wheeled scale measure appears delirious, wandering the wasteland, the barren rolling moors of *Garreg Las*—not the place to be when the weather is bad.

Unwrapping my stoneware beaker, I fill it with hot water from the flask. Turning the form, now warm in my hands, I trace the links between East and West. The grey- green woodash glaze, made from English oak, contrasting with the illustrious, thick, black *Tenmoku*, breaking to rich orange rust over the engraved motif of a willow tree. There is a 'oneness' in the fusion of Japanese folk craft of Shoji Hamada and the English monastic form of Bernard Leach. My thumb explores, with rhythmic caress, the fishtail handle, wiping in the manner of the potter. I make tea—today it is Lapsang Souchong

Suddenly, there is a panting, rushing clatter, out there in the fog, then stumbling between us, two men, camouflaged blackened faces, retching for breath. 'Christ, ' one blasts; wide-eyed we stare at each other, speechless. 'Sorry about this, ' he says apologetically, desperately trying to control his breathing; then, thrusting out his hand, 'Hefin Jones. And this is my mate Chadri.' Chadri beams a broad, white, Nepalese smile. 'Chadri saka, very pleased to meet you, sir;' he says, bowing respect-fully. I introduce myself'...and my son Matthew.' 'Father and son, eh?' Hefin exclaims in that wonderful broad, musical tongue of the Welsh. 'Ruddy marvellous that is, on top of a mountain, in thick fog, taking tea—fair do's, that's ruddy marvellous—do you mind if I smoke?' Hefin unwraps a waterproof packet from his breast pocket, flips open a metal container and, cupping his hands, lights up. He draws hard on the two hand- rolled ciga-rettes, then passing one to Chadri exhorts, 'needed that, ruddy marvellous that is.' They draw deeply in unison and exhale powerfully through flared nostrils, like giant engines getting up steam. The match, still held between Hefin's thumb and finger, a votive talisman, burns down. At the very last moment he gently blows out the flame. The spent match cools, then slowly forms a curve. At peace now, Hefin cradles his AK47, like a mother and child, 'Time to go,' Hefin says calmly. Cigarettes are nipped, both butts and the charred match are placed carefully in the container, wrapped once more and returned to his breast pocket. Hefin slips out of the harness of the 140-litre Bergen that had seemed part of his form and Chadri quickly adjusts the straps to fit his own slight frame. They both check the Bergen, as if preparing for a drop or running up a mountain and across the wasteland of *Garreg Las*. 'Great meeting you both—don't stay too long now and get cold, this smog from the valley is setting in for the day,' says Hefin. We are joined for a moment in warm, firm handshakes, then, 'Right,' barks Hefin. 'Right,' replies Chadri. And they are gone.

'I think Hefin is probably right, Father.' 'May I suggest we make our return journey by way of the *Fan Hir* track, the up-draught from the valley often thins the mist along the cliff edge.' Writing three short lines on a flat stone fragment, I place it a couple of layers down in the cairn. The mountain mist swirls around us as we leave . . . together.

> white out—
> the croaks of ravens
> become the mountain

Linda Jeannette Ward :::

Competency

THE MENTAL HEALTH CLINIC that serves this small community still relies on the charity of its populace to provide needed space for the occasional evaluation I'm asked to do: In an 1890s church cradled in a curve of live oaks even older we sit in a borrowed room, a scarred card table between us. The court report says she's become paranoid, phoning up deputies into the night with tales of prowlers that never materialize . . . but I wonder—isn't her four-room ramshackle dwelling a remnant of time before development crowded in? I know the place, seen it squeezed in over the years by McDonald's, gas stations, quick stop shops; and groups of bored teens might find it thrilling to spook the old black lady. Her hand-lettered *No Trespassing* sign sits slantwise by the front door, and she can sometimes be seen from the buzzing highway that was an unpaved road in her youth. Now, in this place where hymns still drift through Sunday windows, I'm asked by the court to judge her competency . . .

> octogenarian's hand
> crossing paper
> pauses to touch mine . . .
>   a spring breeze whispers
>   through Spanish moss

Haiku ::: Michael McClintock
Image ::: Kuniharu Shimizu

60 stories
of glass:
the summer moon

Pamela Miller Ness ::: Haiku & Image

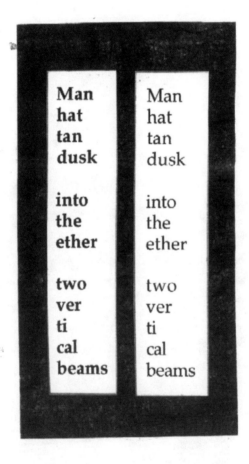

Man
hat
tan
dusk

into
the
ether

two
ver
ti
cal
beams

Man
hat
tan
dusk

into
the
ether

two
ver
ti
cal
beams

Haiku & Image ::: Sam Yada Cannarozzi

```
the                 flakes                    oh
the                 flakes                    oh
the                 flakes                    oh
the                 flakes                    oh
the                 flakes                    oh
                    flakes
snow                flakes                    the
snow                                          the
snow                                          the
snow                                          the
snow                my                        the
                    my
begins              my                        bees
begins              my                        bees
begins              my                        bees
begins              my                        bees
begins              my                        bees

                    daughter                  sting
                    daughter                  sting
big                 daughter                  sting
big                 daughter                  sting
big                 daughter                  sting
big                 daughter
big                                           me
                    exclaims                  me
                    exclaims                  me
                    exclaims                  me
                    exclaims                  me
                    exclaims
                    exclaims
                    exclaims

                                         too
```

Jim Kacian ::: Haiku & Image

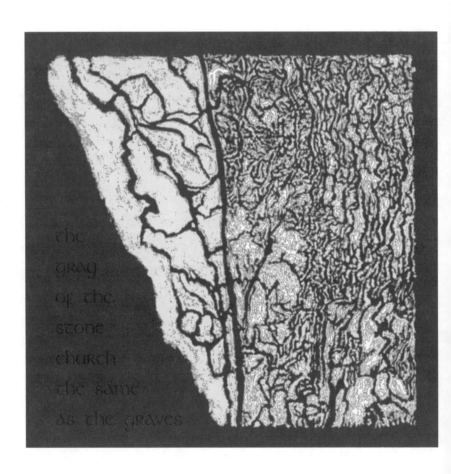

the
gray
of the
stone
church
the same
as the graves

Make a Visual Display of Yourself

I ATTENDED A SEMINAR at the Grand Hyatt Hotel in Union Square. Holiday shoppers abound as Macy's is brightly wrapped inside electronic wreaths. Shoppers use umbrellas to duel with rain as I, and 650 other lucky people, crammed inside the basement of the Grand Hyatt, two escalators down. We'd come to hear Edward Tufte, an information architect par excellence who teaches "by the book, " that is, by all his remarkable books, sharing case studies, visuals, analysis, and scholarship.

He even brought along his personal 430 year-old copy of Euclid's Geometry signed by Ben Jonson. The Fox. An assistant thumbed through pages wearing latex gloves. Only if I had been sitting aisle-side so I could've seen the poet's signature. Instead, I listened to Tufte talk about bulleted lists and how *PowerPoint* presentations corrupt thought by making us substitute strategic for generic thinking, excising narrative from text. Tufte described how low-resolution devices, our small screen world, is causing us to become stupid, removing richness from thought.

Since I spend most of my time in front of one of these devices, what will this make me in the next 10 years? I can't wait to spend time with his gorgeous books and keep the man talking inside my ear to help ward off inevitable idiocy.

Oh, for a heavy ceramic cup of tea.

on the surface
of the steel-and-glass table
Euclid's Geometry

Alison Williams :::

Dust

THE SKY TODAY IS A BRIGHT, LIGHT BLUE. The air as cold and clear as water.

The sun shines on the far end of a wooden shelf where odd things, picked up here and there over the years, lie.

> a small shell
> from another summer
> spirals around
> what used to be
> a secret sanctuary

There is a place that is as empty as the sky, and as full of light. A place of silent music, where time slips. At least, that's how it seems to me. A place where we met, in a way not to be repeated. Sometimes I go back, always alone. These autumn days, when we look into the sky, do we see two sunsets or only one?

> can't stop
> however hard
> I try
> wondering how
> you see it now

A breath of wind and dust motes rise, glinting, then slowly settle back into dullness again.

::: Alison Williams

Scree

AFTER WE WALKED SO FAR. Lying in the cave's mouth, at the top of
the scree slope. Head down, breathing, calm. I know this feel-
ing, this immobility of sleep. I will not, cannot move. Then,
without a word . . . a firm push with one foot begins the slide.
Small rocks begin tumbling, gaining momentum, falling down
the steep slope, turning, falling out of sight.

suddenly awake
gripping nothing
tight

Alison Williams :::

Shadows in the Folds

OUR CHILDREN HAVE NO BODIES. They are paper children, dancing dolls, cut from the white sheets we have written on. Arms outstretched, hands joined each one to the next as they unfold. Singing a song that has no meaning deeper than it's sound.

> birds fly up
> from the dry bed
> of a river

::: Rich Youmans

Head-On

DRIVING TOWARD THE CONCERT, along a backroad dense with insects and pine, we come to the slow procession of cars. It stretches through deepening twilight, disappears around the bend a half mile up. Oh God, I mutter. Accident, my wife says; maybe road work. We close in, join the row of cars. We're going to be late, I say; an hour at least. My wife doesn't answer. White headlights rush us from around the bend— prisoners set free, running wild-eyed into the night. Then they end and, one by one, we begin to move.

> taillights fade
> and flare...
> above, one steady star

We wait. Behind us, headlights accumulate. This is ridiculous, I say, it had been such a nice day—as if that should excuse us from this tie- up. But it had been wonderful, one of those rare Saturdays when everything went right: a morning of small chores accomplished without effort, an afternoon spent watching the Red Sox win, an early dinner at our favorite Thai restaurant, with the anticipation of a performance by the Tokyo String Quartet. Now this. My wife, always the more patient one, hums one of her favorite tunes—something from Bach, a sonatina. It makes me think of our vacant seats, waiting in the concert hall. Five minutes, I report; five minutes and we've barely moved. My wife just continues to hum. A siren grows loud, louder, cuts off. It's not road work, my wife says. I nod, half- listening. Headlights pass.

117

Taillights dim, crawl forward, grow bright again. Twilight turns to night: only a few stars, no moon. Finally, after forty minutes, we begin to round the bend.

red light beating
against the pine—
my pulse

Slowly the scene presents itself: a police car like a battleship across our lane; one officer directing vehicles around a row of red flares. On the roadside, a station wagon, its front end nearly gone, its entire windshield burst; glass glitters across the black-top, as if all the stars had dropped. A rear door is open; near it, three white-shirted medics huddle over a sheeted figure. Farther down, an ambulance and its warm interior light sits parked beneath the pines, cozy as a small house. Head-on, my wife says. They must have already towed the other car. Then she points to a spot just left of the medics, and touches my hand . . .

by the bright flare
a child's sneaker,
its laces still tied

Quickly, it comes to me: the end of an outing; a family return-ing from a picnic, the park; a husband, a wife, children full and sleepy from hot dogs and sun. Wagon running smoothly through the shadows of pines, dotted white line zipping past its tires, windshield filled with the last light of a day suddenly canceled as the family rounds the bend. An officer waves us on, and we proceed past the wagon with its violated metal; past the medics who calmly work, their movements precise and quick; past the white sneaker. Then we are back in our lane, speeding up, passing the stalled row of oncoming cars. We have become one of the wild-eyed ones, yet we do not feel free. My wife no longer hums her favorite Bach, and I have stopped thinking of the concert. Instead, I concentrate on the road, on the insects flicking through the headlight beams. I am conscious of my wife—of her cream- colored dress, her pendant earrings, the curl in her hair. I touch her pale arm, just to feel its skin; she takes my fingers, doesn't let go. Carefully, I steer down the road with one hand, my knuckles white against the wheel, as we proceed through the night.

from star
to star—
the deep space between

Jianqing Zheng :::

Moonlight

IN 1936, JI XIAN, A WELL-KNOWN CHINESE POET who lives now in San Francisco, lived in Suzhou, a garden city in China, but he taught and edited a literary magazine in Shanghai. He commuted happily between the two cities. Each time when Ji Xian came back home, his friend Yao Yingcai, a professor and musical talent in Suzhou, would drop by for a chat and dinner with him. Usually after dinner, Yao, who could memorize almost all of Beethoven's musical pieces, would play *Moonlight* in the living room. One time, Yao even turned off the lights in order to create a musical atmosphere when he played *Moonlight*. Touched by Yao's wonderful performances, Ji Xian imagined:

> The moon rising on the keys;
> The lamp in the dark room.

In 1938 Yao went to the front to fight the invaders and died heroically in the war. Since then, Ji Xian never heard anyone who could play Beethoven's *Moonlight* as well as Yingcai did, because Yingcai's moonlight has been shining in Ji Xian's memory for over sixty years.

> Moonlight—
> Cassia flowers blooming
> In sweet memory

Haiku ::: Carmen Sterba
Image ::: Susan Frame

暖かくて炒る莢豆り
旬たつ

[warmer days / scent of fresh pea pods / in the stir fry]

flood plain
inch by inch shorter
the bulrushes

Haiku ::: Melissa Dixon
Image ::: Susan Frame

[lilies' bowed heads / by the convent gate— / a new memorial tree]

修
道
門
の
百
合
は
垂
れ
さ
り
新
記
念
樹

Gary Gay ::: Haiku
Kuniharu Shimizu ::: Image

Marsh wind,
the whole flock
changes direction

::: Contributors

Acknowledgments :::

Michael McClintock—"Unnatural Amber" *Frogpond* XXV:3

Fay O'Neill—"A Journey to the Outback" *Yellow Moon* 12

Cor van den Heuvel—"Yellow" *Journeys* 1

Lenore Weiss—"Make a Visual Display of Yourself" *Frogpond* XXVI:1